4◐**minute**
BIBLE STUDIES

D0343486

Turning Your Heart Toward God

Kay Arthur, David & BJ Lawson

PRECEPT MINISTRIES INTERNATIONAL

WATERBROOK
PRESS

Turning Your Heart Toward God
Published by WaterBrook Press
12265 Oracle Boulevard, Suite 200
Colorado Springs, Colorado 80921

ISBN 978-0-307-45872-8
ISBN 978-0-307-45873-5 (electronic)

Published in the United States by WaterBrook Multnomah, an imprint of the Crown Publishing Group, a division of Random House Inc., New York.

WaterBrook and its deer colophon are registered trademarks of Random House Inc.

Printed in the United States of America
2010—First Edition

10 9 8 7 6 5 4 3 2 1

Special Sales
Most WaterBrook Multnomah books are available at special quantity discounts when purchased in bulk by corporations, organizations, and special-interest groups. Custom imprinting or excerpting can also be done to fit special needs. For information, please e-mail SpecialMarkets@WaterBrookMultnomah.com or call 1-800-603-7051.

CONTENTS

HOW TO USE THIS STUDY

This small-group study is for people who are interested in learning for themselves more about what the Bible says on various subjects, but who have only limited time to meet together. It's ideal, for example, for a lunch group at work, an early morning men's group, a young mothers' group meeting in a home, a Sunday-school class, or even family devotions. (It's also ideal for small groups that typically have longer meeting times—such as evening groups or Saturday morning groups—but want to devote only a portion of their time together to actual study, while reserving the rest for prayer, fellowship, or other activities.)

This book is designed so that all the group's participants will complete each lesson's study activities *at the same time.* Discussing your insights drawn from what God says about the subject reveals exciting, life-impacting truths.

Although it's a group study, you'll need a facilitator to lead the study and keep the discussion moving. (This person's function is *not* that of a lecturer or teacher. However, when this book is used in a Sunday-school class or similar setting, the teacher should feel free to lead more directly and to bring in other insights in addition to those provided in each week's lesson.)

If *you* are your group's facilitator, the leader, here are some helpful points for making your job easier:

- Go through the lesson and mark the text before you lead the group. This will give you increased familiarity with the material and will enable you to facilitate the group with greater ease. It may be easier for you to lead the group through the instructions for marking if you, as a leader, choose a specific color for each symbol you mark.

- As you lead the group, start at the beginning of the text and simply read it aloud in the order it appears in the lesson, including the "insight boxes," which appear throughout. Work through the lesson together, observing and discussing what you learn. As you read the Scripture verses, have the group say aloud the word they are marking in the text.

- The discussion questions are there simply to help you cover the material. As the class moves into the discussion, many times you will find that they will cover the questions on their own. Remember, the discussion questions are there to guide the group through the topic, not to squelch discussion.

- Remember how important it is for people to verbalize their answers and discoveries. This greatly strengthens their personal understanding of each week's lesson. Try to ensure that everyone has plenty of opportunity to contribute to each week's discussions.

- Keep the discussion moving. This may mean spending more time on some parts of the study than on others. If necessary, you should feel free to spread out a lesson over more than one session. However, remember that you don't want to slow the pace too much. It's much better to leave everyone "wanting more" than to have people dropping out because of declining interest.

- If the validity or accuracy of some of the answers seems questionable, you can gently and cheerfully remind the group to stay focused on the truth of the Scriptures. Your object is to learn what the Bible says, not to engage in human philosophy. Simply stick with the Scriptures and give God the opportunity to speak. His Word *is* truth (John 17:17)!

TURNING YOUR HEART TOWARD GOD

C ertain events and moments in time have changed the course of history. A few, a precious few, have even changed the course of eternity. Take for example the birth, the death, and the resurrection of Jesus Christ. His life changed not only history but even eternity.

Jesus' delivery of the Sermon on the Mount is one of those pivotal events. In what is now undoubtedly the most famous sermon in the world Jesus took righteousness to a whole new level, all in one fell swoop. He defined religion in a way that was then, and is still today, countercultural, radical, and even revolutionary.

The sermon itself can be preached word-for-word in eighteen minutes, but you could spend a lifetime studying it and never completely search out its depths. The introduction alone—the subject of numerous books, essays, and discussions—is so powerful, so inspiring that it carries its own name exclusive of the Sermon on the Mount: *The Beatitudes.* In these few verses Jesus introduces the core belief system that changed the world.

As you study what it means to be blessed of God and how those blessings are manifest in our lives, you will see that this is the practical side of living in a real world. As we live out the blessings, we become a light shining in the darkness, a city set on a hill that cannot be hidden. We become ambassadors for the Son of God.

We then have the opportunity to impact world—all because we studied the introduction to a two-thousand-year-old sermon.

Do you want to be blessed by God? Well, of course. We all do. We want His blessing in our lives. This week we will define, from Scripture, the word *blessed* and we will study the first beatitude to see who it is that receives the blessing of God. Start with prayer. Before we get into the study, let's spend some time in prayer, asking God to help us see these familiar verses with a heart open to His truth.

OBSERVE

Matthew 5–7 is commonly called the Sermon on the Mount. Jesus began His sermon with the Beatitudes.

Leader: Read Matthew 5:1–12 aloud. Have the group say aloud and mark...
- *every reference to **Jesus,** including pronouns, with a cross:* †
- *draw a box around each occurrence of the word **blessed:*** ☐

As you read the text, it's helpful to have the group say the key words aloud as they mark them. This way everyone will be sure they are marking every occurrence of the word, including any synonymous words or phrases. Do this throughout the study.

MATTHEW 5:1–12

¹ When Jesus saw the crowds, He went up on the mountain; and after He sat down, His disciples came to Him.

² He opened His mouth and began to teach them, saying,

³ "Blessed are the poor in spirit, for theirs is the kingdom of heaven.

⁴ "Blessed are those who mourn, for they shall be comforted.

5 "Blessed are the gentle, for they shall inherit the earth.

6 "Blessed are those who hunger and thirst for righteousness, for they shall be satisfied.

7 "Blessed are the merciful, for they shall receive mercy.

8 "Blessed are the pure in heart, for they shall see God.

9 "Blessed are the peacemakers, for they shall be called sons of God.

10 "Blessed are those who have been persecuted for the sake of righteousness, for theirs is the kingdom of heaven.

11 "Blessed are you when people insult

DISCUSS

• What did you learn from marking *Jesus*?

• Who was Jesus teaching?

• What did He start each statement with?

you and persecute you, and falsely say all kinds of evil against you because of Me.

12 "Rejoice and be glad, for your reward in heaven is great; for in the same way they persecuted the prophets who were before you."

OBSERVE

Let's look at what the word *blessed* means.

Leader: Read 1 Timothy 1:11; 6:13–15; and Titus 2:11–13 aloud.
• *Have the group say aloud and draw a box around each occurrence of the word* **blessed.**

1 TIMOTHY 1:11; 6:13–15

11 according to the glorious gospel of the blessed God, with which I have been entrusted....

13 I charge you in the presence of God, who gives life to all things, and of Christ Jesus, who testified the good confession before Pontius Pilate,

DISCUSS

• Who is the word *blessed* associated with in each of these passages?

14 that you keep the commandment without

stain or reproach until the appearing of our Lord Jesus Christ,

15 which He will bring about at the proper time—He who is the blessed and only Sovereign, the King of kings and Lord of lords.

TITUS 2:11–13

11 For the grace of God has appeared, bringing salvation to all men,

12 instructing us to deny ungodliness and worldly desires and to live sensibly, righteously and godly in the present age,

13 looking for the blessed hope and the appearing of the glory of our great God and Savior, Christ Jesus.

• Who is *blessed* characteristic of?

• *Blessed* or *blessedness* is first and foremost a characteristic of God. It is part of who He is, His state of being. What difference does this make to your understanding of us as believers being blessed?

OBSERVE

The Greek word for *blessed—makarios—*is also used in the Septuagint, a Greek translation of the Hebrew Old Testament completed approximately 100 BC. By looking at passages where the ancient translators used *makarios,* we gain insight regarding what they understood the word to mean.

Leader: Read aloud the verses on pages 7 and 8.
  • Have the group say aloud and draw a box around each occurrence of the word **blessed.**

INSIGHT

The Greek word translated *blessed* is *makarios.* It is sometimes translated as happy, but it carries a much deeper meaning. In English the idea of being happy is based on favorable circumstances. But to be blessed is to possess the favor of God. It is a state of being defined by fullness and satisfaction from God. To be blessed is to be walking in the fullness of God regardless of circumstances.

PSALM 1:1–2

1 How blessed is the man who does not walk in the counsel of the wicked, nor stand in the path of sinners, nor sit in the seat of scoffers!

2 But his delight is in the law of the LORD, and in His law he meditates day and night.

PSALM 32:1–2

1 How blessed is he whose transgression is forgiven, whose sin is covered!

2 How blessed is the man to whom the LORD does not impute iniquity, and in whose spirit there is no deceit!

PSALM 34:8

Taste and see that the LORD is good; how blessed is the man who takes refuge in Him!

PSALM 65:4

How blessed is the one whom You choose and bring near to You to dwell in Your courts. We will be satisfied with the goodness of Your house, Your holy temple.

DISCUSS

• Looking at each place you marked *blessed,* what do you notice about the person who is blessed?

• What difference do these descriptions make in your understanding of Jesus' use of the word in the Beatitudes?

• Are you, by these definitions, *blessed*? If not, why not?

OBSERVE

Leader: *Read Matthew 5:3 aloud. Have the group say and...*
  • *draw a box around the word* **blessed.**
  • *draw a cloud shape like this* ⌒⌒⌒
    around the phrase **kingdom of heaven.**

DISCUSS

• Who is blessed, according to this verse?

MATTHEW 5:3

Blessed are the poor in spirit, for theirs is the kingdom of heaven.

INSIGHT

The Greek word translated in Matthew 5:3 as *poor* means "to be poverty stricken, powerless, utterly destitute, and bankrupt." To be "poor in spirit" means knowing you have nothing to offer and acknowledging your total dependence on God. It suggests a humility, which is the opposite of pride.

• Discuss what being poor in spirit would look like in the life of a believer.

• What is promised to those who are poor in spirit?

LUKE 18:9–14

⁹ And He also told this parable to some people who trusted in themselves that they were righteous, and viewed others with contempt:

¹⁰ "Two men went up into the temple to pray, one a Pharisee and the other a tax collector.

¹¹ "The Pharisee stood and was praying this to himself: 'God, I thank You that I am not like other people: swindlers, unjust, adulterers, or even like this tax collector.

¹² 'I fast twice a week; I pay tithes of all that I get.'

OBSERVE

In the gospel of Luke, Jesus gives us a great illustration of what it looks like to be poor in spirit.

Leader: Read Luke 18:9–14 aloud. Have the group…
- *mark every reference to **the Pharisee**, including synonyms and pronouns, with a big **P**.*
- *mark every reference to **the tax collector**, including synonyms and pronouns, with a dollar sign, like this: **$***

DISCUSS

- What did you learn from marking the references to the Pharisee?

- According to verse 11, what was his prayer?

- What did he trust in?

- Verse 13 begins with the word *but,* which often indicates a contrast is being made. Who is the contrast between in these verses?

• What did you learn from marking the references to the tax collector?

• What was the difference between the two men?

• Who was the Pharisee using to measure his righteousness?

• Who did the tax collector use as his standard for measuring righteousness?

• Discuss how this parable illustrates what it means to be poor in spirit.

• Have you ever really seen your poverty of spirit? Have you recognized your inability to meet God's standards? Explain your answer.

13 "But the tax collector, standing some distance away, was even unwilling to lift up his eyes to heaven, but was beating his breast, saying, 'God, be merciful to me, the sinner!'

14 "I tell you, this man went to his house justified rather than the other; for everyone who exalts himself will be humbled, but he who humbles himself will be exalted."

PSALM 34:18

The LORD is near to the brokenhearted and saves those who are crushed in spirit.

PSALM 51:17

The sacrifices of God are a broken spirit; a broken and a contrite heart, O God, You will not despise.

OBSERVE

Look at the following Old Testament verses and note how they would relate to what you have seen so far about being poor in spirit.

Leader: Read Psalm 34:18 and 51:17 aloud.

> *• Have the group say and mark every mention of God, including synonyms and pronouns, with a triangle: △*

DISCUSS

• What did you learn about God in these verses?

• How do these insights relate to what we have been studying?

OBSERVE

Leader: Read Isaiah 57:15 aloud. Have the group...

- *mark every synonym and pronoun referring to **God** with a triangle.*
- *underline each occurrence of the words **lowly** and **contrite.***

DISCUSS

- What did you learn from marking the references to God?

- What does He want to do for the lowly and contrite of spirit?

- How does that relate to what Jesus said about the poor in spirit?

ISAIAH 57:15

For thus says the high and exalted One Who lives forever, whose name is Holy, "I dwell on a high and holy place, and also with the contrite and lowly of spirit in order to revive the spirit of the lowly and to revive the heart of the contrite.

ISAIAH 66:1–2

1 Thus says the LORD, "Heaven is My throne and the earth is My footstool. Where then is a house you could build for Me? And where is a place that I may rest?

2 "For My hand made all these things, thus all these things came into being," declares the LORD. "But to this one I will look, to him who is humble and contrite of spirit, and who trembles at My word."

OBSERVE

In Isaiah's day the people were going through the motions of worship without having a heart for God.

Leader: Read Isaiah 66:1–2 aloud. Have the group say aloud and...

- *mark each reference to **the Lord,** including pronouns, with a triangle.*
- *underline the phrase **humble and contrite of spirit.***

DISCUSS

- What did you learn about the Lord in these verses?

- What does God look for in a person?

OBSERVE

After Matthew, a tax collector, began to follow Jesus, he held a dinner at his house.

Leader: Read Matthew 9:10–13 aloud. Have the group...
- *mark each reference to **Jesus**, including pronouns, with a cross:* †
- *mark every reference to **the Pharisees**, including synonyms and pronouns, with a big* **P.**

DISCUSS

- Who had Matthew invited to dinner?

- Why do you think he may have invited this particular group of people?

MATTHEW 9:10–13

10 Then it happened that as Jesus was reclining at the table in the house, behold, many tax collectors and sinners came and were dining with Jesus and His disciples.

11 When the Pharisees saw this, they said to His disciples, "Why is your Teacher eating with the tax collectors and sinners?"

12 But when Jesus heard this, He said, "It is not those who are healthy who need a physician, but those who are sick.

13 "But go and learn what this means: 'I

desire compassion, and not sacrifice,' for I did not come to call the righteous, but sinners."

• How did the Pharisees react to this scene?

• Keeping in mind that the Pharisees were the religious leaders of the day, why do you think they responded in this way?

• What did Jesus' words demonstrate? Who did He come to call?

• What did Jesus tell the people to do in verse 13, and why? How does it relate to the previous verses?

OBSERVE

At one point early in His earthly ministry, Jesus returned to His hometown of Nazareth and went to the synagogue, where He was asked to read from the book of Isaiah.

Leader: Read Luke 4:18–21 aloud. Have the group…

• *mark each reference to **Jesus**, including pronouns, with a cross.*

• *underline the phrase **to proclaim the favorable year of the Lord.***

DISCUSS

• What ministries had Jesus been anointed to do?

• Do you see any possible parallel between this passage and what we have seen about being poor in Spirit? Explain your answer.

INSIGHT

The portion of Scripture Jesus read was Isaiah 61:1–2, a messianic passage. By adding "Today this Scripture is fulfilled in your hearing," Jesus claimed to be the Messiah who would bring in the long-promised kingdom of God.

LUKE 4:18–21

18 "The Spirit of the Lord is upon Me, because He anointed Me to preach the gospel to the poor. He has sent Me to proclaim release to the captives, and recovery of sight to the blind, to set free those who are oppressed,

19 To proclaim the favorable year of the Lord."

20 And He closed the book, gave it back to the attendant and sat down; and the eyes of all in the synagogue were fixed on Him.

21 And He began to say to them, "Today this Scripture has been fulfilled in your hearing."

PHILIPPIANS 3:4–9

4 although I myself might have confidence even in the flesh. If anyone else has a mind to put confidence in the flesh, I far more:

5 circumcised the eighth day, of the nation of Israel, of the tribe of Benjamin, a Hebrew of Hebrews; as to the Law, a Pharisee;

6 as to zeal, a persecutor of the church; as to the righteousness which is in the Law, found blameless.

7 But whatever things were gain to me, those things I have counted as loss for the sake of Christ.

8 More than that, I count all things to be

OBSERVE

As we bring this lesson to a close, let's take a look at how the apostle Paul demonstrated poverty of spirit.

Leader: Read Philippians 3:4–9 aloud. Have the group say and...

- *circle each occurrence of the pronoun* Ⓘ *which refers in this passage to* ***Paul.***
- *draw a squiggly line like this* 〰 *under each of these phrases:* ***counted as loss, to be loss, suffered the loss,*** *and* ***count them but rubbish.***
- *mark each occurrence of the word* ***righteousness*** *with a big* **R.**

DISCUSS

- What did you learn about Paul in verses 4–6?

• Verse 7 starts with the word *but,* which, as we've seen, often indicates a contrast is being made. What contrast was Paul making in verses 7 and 8?

loss in view of the surpassing value of knowing Christ Jesus my Lord, for whom I have suffered the loss of all things, and count them but rubbish so that I may gain Christ,

9 and may be found in Him, not having a righteousness of my own derived from the Law, but that which is through faith in Christ, the righteousness which comes from God on the basis of faith.

• For what reason was Paul counting these things as loss and what would the result be?

• What are the two different kinds of righteousness described by Paul?

• Which righteousness did Paul place his confidence in?

• Paul counted or considered the things in his life and made the decision not to cling to any righteousness of his own. Have you done that?

• Can you identify any factors in your life that may be keeping you from seeing your true poverty of spirit? What are they? Wealth? Worldly wisdom? Strong natural abilities? Your own righteousness?

Leader: *If time allows, take this opportunity to lead the group in a time of prayer and reflection.*

WRAP IT UP

It seems to be ingrained in our human nature to think that we are better than perhaps we really are. This is especially true when it comes to standing before the Righteous Judge of the universe. All too often, when it comes to sin, we justify our actions by comparing ourselves to someone we believe is worse than we are. It's as if we believe God grades us on a curve. *Sure,* we tell ourselves, *I'm not perfect, but I look pretty good compared to that other person.*

The Pharisee from Jesus' parable in Luke 18 saw himself that way. Compared to others, he judged himself to be a pretty good guy, far more righteous than the average, ordinary sinner.

But that's not the way God judges. His standard is perfection, not goodness. Romans 3:10 tells us, "There is none righteous, not even one." No one measures up to the standard known as righteousness. Paul goes on to say in Romans 3:23, "For all have sinned and fall short of the glory of God." We all have come short of the standard.

As you saw this week, our only hope for blessing is to admit our utter dependence on God. "God is opposed the proud, but gives grace to the humble" (1 Peter 5:5). Those who are walking in the fullness of God, those whose inheritance is heaven are those who are poor in spirit. Only the ones who realize that they have no righteousness of their own to offer God will inherit the kingdom of heaven.

Put yourself in the parable of Luke 18. Who are you? Deep down in your heart, deep in your soul, which man do you resemble?

God be merciful to us, the sinners!

Ask God to show you your poverty of spirit so that you can find fullness in Him.

"Blessed are those who mourn." *Really?* Taken at face value, that statement seems strange. However, we learned last week that it is the poor in spirit who are blessed, that when we reach the point of realizing our spiritual bankruptcy we are able to be blessed of God.

Since Jesus immediately followed up that beatitude with a statement about mourning, maybe there is a connection between mourning and realizing our poverty of spirit. May you gain a deeper understanding of what it means to be blessed through this week's study.

OBSERVE

Leader: *Read Matthew 5:4 aloud. Have the group say aloud and...*

- *draw a box around the word **blessed:***

- *mark the word **mourn** with a teardrop, like this:* ◯

MATTHEW 5:4

Blessed are those who mourn, for they shall be comforted.

DISCUSS

- Who is blessed in this verse?

INSIGHT

The specific language used in this verse includes the strongest word for mourning in the Greek language. It is the term used for mourning the death of a loved one, and it describes a grief that cannot be hidden.

PSALM 34:17–18

17 The righteous cry, and the LORD hears and delivers them out of all their troubles.

18 The LORD is near to the brokenhearted and saves those who are crushed in spirit.

PSALM 147:3

He heals the brokenhearted and binds up their wounds.

OBSERVE

Leader: Read Psalm 34:17–18 and Psalm 147:3 aloud.

• *Have the group say aloud and mark each occurrence of the word* **brokenhearted** *and the phrase* **crushed in spirit** *with a teardrop:* ⬯

DISCUSS

• What did you learn about those who are brokenhearted or crushed in spirit?

• How does this relate to Matthew 5:4, "Blessed are those who mourn, for they shall be comforted"?

OBSERVE

Jesus said, "Blessed are those who mourn." The question is, what are we to mourn? To help us understand what Jesus meant, let's look at another place in the Scriptures where this word *mourn* is used.

Leader: Read James 4:6–10 aloud. Have the group...
- *underline each **instruction.** Watch for the action words.*
- *mark each occurrence of **mourn** and **mourning** with a teardrop.*

DISCUSS

• How are we to humble ourselves before God? Make a list of the instructions you underlined.

• According to James, how does one draw near to God? What sort of things should we do?

• How is it possible to remove the barrier between man and God?

JAMES 4:6–10

6 But He gives a greater grace. Therefore it says, "God is opposed to the proud, but gives grace to the humble."

7 Submit therefore to God. Resist the devil and he will flee from you.

8 Draw near to God and He will draw near to you. Cleanse your hands, you sinners; and purify your hearts, you double-minded.

9 Be miserable and mourn and weep; let your laughter be turned into mourning and your joy to gloom.

10 Humble yourselves in the presence of the Lord, and He will exalt you.

INSIGHT

Both *cleanse* and *purify* are technical terms in the Old Testament that refer to the ceremonial cleansing of the priests (Exodus 30:19–21). The reference to cleansing, which brings to mind an external action such as hand washing, would indicate stopping certain behaviors. The admonition to "purify your heart" deals more with the internal cleansing of an individual's thoughts, motives, and desires of the heart.

The *double-minded* man suffers from divided loyalties. On one hand he desires to be near to and please God; on the other he loves the world and all it has to offer.

• What is to be our response to sin?

• If we respond correctly to sin, what will God do? How does that relate to this particular beatitude?

• When was the last time you truly mourned over your sin? The sin of others?

• According to what you saw in Matthew 5:4, what can those who mourn over sin expect?

• Examine your heart. Discuss what it means to be double minded and how it relates to this week's study.

OBSERVE

In response to sin in the church at Corinth, the apostle Paul wrote a harsh letter of discipline and sent it with Titus. Though it caused pain to both Paul and the Corinthian believers, the letter achieved its purpose.

Leader: *Read 2 Corinthians 7:8–10 aloud. Have the group…*
> • *mark each reference to **sorrow** or **sorrowful** with a teardrop.*
> • *underline each occurrence of the phrase **according to the will of God.***

2 CORINTHIANS 7:8–10

8 For though I caused you sorrow by my letter, I do not regret it; though I did regret it—for I see that that letter caused you sorrow, though only for a while—

9 I now rejoice, not that you were made sorrowful, but that you

were made sorrowful to the point of repentance; for you were made sorrowful according to the will of God, so that you might not suffer loss in anything through us.

10 For the sorrow that is according to the will of God produces a repentance without regret, leading to salvation, but the sorrow of the world produces death.

DISCUSS

• What did you learn from marking the references to sorrow?

• Why was Paul rejoicing?

• How was the church's sorrow connected to God's will?

• In verse 10, Paul draws a contrast between two kinds of sorrow. What are they, and in what way(s) are they different?

INSIGHT

Repentance means changing your mind about your sin and bringing your actions in line with God's will.

• Have you ever received a rebuke over your sin? How did it make you feel? What was the end result?

OBSERVE

In another of his letters to the Corinthians, Paul dealt with issues in the church, including their failure to discipline a brother in sin.

Leader: Read 1 Corinthians 5:1–2 aloud. Have the group say and...

- *circle each occurrence of the pronoun ⟨you⟩ which refers to the Corinthians in this verses.*
- *mark the word mourned with a teardrop.*

DISCUSS

- What issue was Paul addressing? From what you have read, how serious was it?

- If this situation was not dealt with, what impact would it have on the church?

1 CORINTHIANS 5:1–2

1 It is actually reported that there is immorality among you, and immorality of such a kind as does not exist even among the Gentiles, that someone has his father's wife.

2 You have become arrogant and have not mourned instead, so that the one who had done this deed would be removed from your midst.

• How had the Corinthians responded to this shameful situation?

• What should have been their response?

• Have you heard of a church or even a denomination that was so "loving" and "welcoming" they never challenged or really even acknowledged any sin in the body? How does that compare with Paul's instruction to the Corinthians for dealing with sin?

2 CORINTHIANS 12:20–21

20 For I am afraid that perhaps when I come I may find you to be not what I wish and may be found by you to be not what you wish; that perhaps there will be strife, jealousy, angry tem-

OBSERVE

Paul wrote of wanting to visit once more the church at Corinth, but he had some concerns.

Leader: Read 2 Corinthians 12:20–21 aloud. Have the group...

> • *circle each of the pronouns **I** and **me**, which refer to **Paul** in these verses.*
> • *mark the word **mourn** with a teardrop.*

DISCUSS

• What was Paul afraid he would find if he visited the church at Corinth?

• What would Paul mourn over in this church?

• Sins in the church must be faced honestly and dealt with courageously. Paul's love for the Corinthians did not prevent him from challenging their sins. It caused him to mourn their sin. Do you mourn over sin? Or will you simply overlook it? Consider your answer prayerfully.

• Does your church, your Christian community, mourn over sin or simply overlook it? Explain your answer.

pers, disputes, slanders, gossip, arrogance, disturbances;

21 I am afraid that when I come again my God may humiliate me before you, and I may mourn over many of those who have sinned in the past and not repented of the impurity, immorality and sensuality which they have practiced.

WRAP IT UP

"Like the Holy One who called you, be holy yourselves also in all your behavior; because it is written, 'You shall be holy, for I am holy'" (1 Peter 1:15–16).

Holiness is the standard. Each of us is to be holy just as God is holy. Let that soak in for a moment. Holiness is the goal. Sound impossible? You might be thinking it was possible for some saint back in history, but not now, not today. Maybe you feel that you just don't have it in you to be holy. You could try, but deep down, you suspect you just wouldn't make it.

Good news! Blessed are the poor in spirit. Blessed are the ones who realize they just don't have it in them to be holy. They are blessed because they are the ones God helps. God helps the helpless.

As we see our spiritual poverty, the Holy Spirit works in us to bring us to mourn over our lack of holiness. God has called us to be holy, and Jesus paid a high and painful price for our un-holiness. Our sin, our lack of holiness, hurts God and it hurts the people around us.

The natural response to sin is to ignore it, rationalizing that no one is perfect. Sometimes we justify sin by blaming someone else. And sometimes we place happiness above holiness, reasoning that we just want people to feel accepted.

The supernatural response to sin, the response prompted by the Holy Spirit, is to mourn over sin. We should mourn because sin caused the death of the One who loved us unconditionally. Sin hurts God and it causes damage to His people. Therefore we should mourn over our sin and the sins of others.

Spend some time in prayer today, asking God to break your heart with the things that break His. Ask Him to help you mourn over sin.

Jesus said, "Blessed are the gentle," but realistically, that just doesn't seem to be the case, does it? Those who are aggressive, the fighters, the intellectuals, or even the just plain lucky might inherit the earth. But the gentle can't expect to get ahead, can they?

However, you have seen in the first two lessons that Jesus' view of life and righteousness is nothing like the world's perspective. The biblical view of gentleness is not what you may have expected either.

In this lesson we will see who the gentle are and what it means for them to inherit the earth.

OBSERVE

Leader: Read Matthew 5:5 aloud. Have the group say aloud and...
- *draw a box around the word* **blessed.**
- *draw a squiggly line like this* ～～～ *under the word* **gentle.**

MATTHEW 5:5

Blessed are the gentle, for they shall inherit the earth.

DISCUSS

• Who is blessed, according to Matthew 5:5?

• What will be the result?

INSIGHT

The ancient Greeks understood the gentle or meek person to be the one who is angry on the right occasion, with the right people, at the right moment, for the right amount of time. Aristotle, for example, defined it as the middle point between excessive anger and the inability to show anger. This is very different than our modern understanding of gentleness.

PSALM 37:1–11

¹ Do not fret because of evildoers, be not envious toward wrongdoers.

² For they will wither quickly like the grass and fade like the green herb.

³ Trust in the LORD and do good; dwell in the land and cultivate faithfulness.

OBSERVE

Although it doesn't quite look like it in the New American Standard Bible, the translation we're using here, Matthew 5:5 is a direct quote from the Septuagint of Psalm 37:11. Let's look at that verse in its full context to see how meekness responds under fire.

Leader: Read Psalm 37:1–11 aloud. Have the group do the following:
> • *mark each occurrence of the phrase **do not fret** with a big* **X**.

- *draw a box around each occurrence of the phrase **inherit the land.***
- *draw a squiggly line under the word **humble.***

INSIGHT

As you learned in lesson 1, the Greek translation of the Old Testament is called the Septuagint. Sometimes it is helpful to look at Old Testament passages to see how and where these ancient translators used a Greek word. In the following passages the Greek word for *gentleness* is used in the Septuagint, but in our English version it is translated as *humble*.

DISCUSS

- How should we respond when others seem to be getting away with evil deeds, according to verses 3–4? Who or what should we trust in?

- Because of that trust, what does verse 5 say we should do?

4 Delight yourself in the LORD; and He will give you the desires of your heart.

5 Commit your way to the LORD, trust also in Him, and He will do it.

6 He will bring forth your righteousness as the light and your judgment as the noonday.

7 Rest in the LORD and wait patiently for Him; do not fret because of him who prospers in his way, because of the man who carries out wicked schemes.

8 Cease from anger and forsake wrath; do not fret; it leads only to evildoing.

9 For evildoers will be cut off, but those who wait for the LORD, they will inherit the land.

10 Yet a little while and the wicked man will be no more; and you will look carefully for his place and he will not be there.

11 But the humble will inherit the land and will delight themselves in abundant prosperity.

• Discuss what you learned in verses 6–8.

• In verse 9 the word *but* is used to show that a contrast is being made. The contrast here is between the evildoers and those who wait for the Lord. What did you learn about each of these groups?

• In verses 10–11 we see another contrast. Discuss the contrast and what it reveals about the humble.

• What did you learn about those who will inherit the land?

• How does this relate to what we have seen so far in this lesson?

OBSERVE

Joseph's brothers had plotted his death and then sold him into slavery. Years later, Joseph was second in command of Egypt when his brothers stood before him. Let's see how he dealt with them.

Leader: Read Genesis 50:19–20 aloud. Have the group...
- *mark every reference to **Joseph,** including pronouns, with a big **J.***
- *mark every reference to **God** with a triangle:* △

GENESIS 50:19–20

19 But Joseph said to them, "Do not be afraid, for am I in God's place?

20 "As for you, you meant evil against me, but God meant it for good in order to bring about this present result, to preserve many people alive."

DISCUSS

- Joseph suffered tremendously at the hand of his brothers, yet how did he respond them?

- How was he able to do this?

- How do his actions compare with what you saw in Psalm 37:7?

• By looking beyond his brothers' actions to the sovereignty of God, Joseph was able to choose gentleness rather than anger. Gentleness is not weakness; it is power under control! What about you? Are you walking in gentleness?

JAMES 1:19–21

19 This you know, my beloved brethren. But everyone must be quick to hear, slow to speak and slow to anger;

20 for the anger of man does not achieve the righteousness of God.

21 Therefore, putting aside all filthiness and all that remains of wickedness, in humility receive the word implanted, which is able to save your souls.

OBSERVE

Let's look at the following passages to see what more we can learn about humility.

Leader: Read James 1:19–21 and 1 Peter 3:3–4 aloud. Have the group do the following:
- *circle each occurrence of the word **anger**.*
- *draw a squiggly line under the words **humility** and **gentle**.*
- *mark the word **therefore** with an arrow, like this:* →

DISCUSS

• What did you learn from marking *anger* in James 1:20?

• What does the word *therefore* in verse 21 indicate we should do, and why?

1 PETER 3:3–4

3 Your adornment must not be merely external—braiding the hair, and wearing gold jewelry, or putting on dresses;

• First Peter 3:3–4 addresses wives. According to these verses, how should a woman adorn herself?

4 but let it be the hidden person of the heart, with the imperishable quality of a gentle and quiet spirit, which is precious in the sight of God.

• To put it another way, which of these adornments is precious to God?

• Drawing on all you have learned so far, discuss how a gentle and quiet spirit would be demonstrated in a wife's behavior.

GALATIANS 5:22–23

22 But the fruit of the Spirit is love, joy, peace, patience, kindness, goodness, faithfulness,

23 gentleness, self-control; against such things there is no law.

OBSERVE

Where does gentleness come from?

Leader: Read Galatians 5:22–23 aloud. Have the group…
- *draw a cloud shape like this around **the Spirit.***
- *draw a squiggly line under the word **gentleness.***

DISCUSS

- Where does gentleness come from? Is it something we have to drum up? Explain your answer.

GALATIANS 6:1

Brethren, even if anyone is caught in any trespass, you who are spiritual, restore such a one in a spirit of gentleness; each one looking to yourself, so that you too will not be tempted.

OBSERVE

How is gentleness to be demonstrated in our dealings with others?

Leader: Read Galatians 6:1 and 2 Timothy 2:24–26 aloud.
- *Have the group say aloud and draw a squiggly line under each occurrence of the word **gentleness.***

DISCUSS

- With what similar problem do these two passages deal?

- Discuss what you learned about the role of gentleness in disciplining others. How might you apply this in practical ways with fellow believers? with children? with the lost?

- No matter how horrendous the sin or how strong the snare of Satan, what is to characterize our correction of others? Even if you are angry about someone's sin, how are you to respond?

- Why is this response so important? Explain your answer.

2 TIMOTHY 2:24–26

24 The Lord's bond-servant must not be quarrelsome, but be kind to all, able to teach, patient when wronged,

25 with gentleness correcting those who are in opposition, if perhaps God may grant them repentance leading to the knowledge of the truth,

26 and they may come to their senses and escape from the snare of the devil, having been held captive by him to do his will.

NUMBERS 12:1–13

1 Then Miriam and Aaron spoke against Moses because of the Cushite woman whom he had married (for he had married a Cushite woman);

2 and they said, "Has the LORD indeed spoken only through Moses? Has He not spoken through us as well?" And the LORD heard it.

3 (Now the man Moses was very humble, more than any man who was on the face of the earth.)

4 Suddenly the LORD said to Moses and Aaron and to Miriam, "You three come out to the tent of meeting." So the three of them came out.

OBSERVE

While Moses was leading the Israelites in the wilderness, the people were struck by a plague. Moses' older brother and sister, Aaron and Miriam, challenged his leadership. How did he respond?

Leader: Read Numbers 12:1–13 aloud. Have the group…
- *circle each reference to Moses, including pronouns.*
- *draw a squiggly line under the word humble.*

DISCUSS

- What did you learn about Moses in this passage?

• What can you find in the text about Moses' response to their accusations? What does this suggest to you about his character?

5 Then the LORD came down in a pillar of cloud and stood at the doorway of the tent, and He called Aaron and Miriam. When they had both come forward,

6 He said, "Hear now My words: If there is a prophet among you, I, the LORD, shall make Myself known to him in a vision. I shall speak with him in a dream.

• How did God respond?

7 "Not so, with My servant Moses, He is faithful in all My household;

• What did you learn about gentleness from Moses' example in verse 13?

8 With him I speak mouth to mouth, even openly, and not in dark sayings, and he beholds the form of the LORD. Why then were you not afraid to speak against My servant, against Moses?"

9 So the anger of the LORD burned against them and He departed.

10 But when the cloud had withdrawn from over the tent, behold, Miriam was leprous, as white as snow. As Aaron turned toward Miriam, behold, she was leprous.

11 Then Aaron said to Moses, "Oh, my lord, I beg you, do not account this sin to us, in which we have acted foolishly and in which we have sinned.

12 "Oh, do not let her be like one dead, whose flesh is half

• Have you ever been unjustly attacked or falsely accused? How did you respond?

• Keeping in mind all you have learned this week, how should you respond in the future?

• If you can, share with the group a recent incident when you chose to respond in gentleness to someone's unkind actions. How did you manage it? What was the outcome?

eaten away when he comes from his mother's womb!"

13 Moses cried out to the LORD, saying, "O God, heal her, I pray!"

OBSERVE

"Blessed are the gentle, for they shall inherit the earth." We have looked at what it means to be gentle. Now let's take a look at the inheritance of those who are gentle.

Leader: Read Psalm 37:22, 29 and 34 aloud. Have the group…
- *circle all references to the righteous, including synonyms and pronouns.*
- *underline each occurrence of the phrase inherit the land.*

DISCUSS

• What did you learn about the righteous?

PSALM 37:22, 29, 34

22 For those blessed by Him will inherit the land, but those cursed by Him will be cut off.…

29 The righteous will inherit the land and dwell in it forever.…

34 Wait for the Lord and keep His way, and He will exalt you to inherit the land; when the wicked are cut off, you will see it.

ROMANS 8:16–17

16 The Spirit Himself testifies with our spirit that we are children of God,

17 and if children, heirs also, heirs of God and fellow heirs with Christ, if indeed we suffer with Him so that we may also be glorified with Him.

OBSERVE

Let's take a look at a New Testament parallel to Psalm 37.

Leader: Read Romans 8:16–17 aloud. Have the group…
- *circle the pronouns **our** and **we**, which refer to **believers**.*
- *mark each occurrence of the word **heirs** with a big **H**.*

DISCUSS

• What did you learn about believers?

• What are they heirs of? What does that mean?

OBSERVE

In the book of Revelation, John wrote of a song sung in heaven in praise of the Lamb that was slain.

Leader: Read Revelation 5:9–10 aloud. Have the group…
  - *all the pronouns that refer to **Jesus** with a cross:* †
  - *circle each reference to **men**, including pronouns.*

DISCUSS

• What did you learn from marking the references to Jesus?

• What did you learn about those who have been purchased by His blood?

REVELATION 5:9–10

9 And they sang a new song, saying, "Worthy are You to take the book and to break its seals; for You were slain, and purchased for God with Your blood men from every tribe and tongue and people and nation.

10 "You have made them to be a kingdom and priests to our God; and they will reign upon the earth."

WRAP IT UP

A horse that has learned to accept direction from its master is a picture of power under control—the definition of gentleness. In a similar way, we will never be really, biblically gentle until we have surrendered our will to the will of God. To put it another way, strength without control leads to chaos, like a river raging at flood stage. But gentleness is seen in that same river channeled through a dam, spinning turbines and creating electricity.

Gentleness starts with unconditional surrender to the control of God. Have you ever given your will to God? Have you ever cried out to Him and said, *Not my will be done, but Yours?* When you do, gentleness becomes something He works within you, not something you must try to manufacture on your own.

The mistake we make all too often is trying to live the Christian life on our terms, in our own strength, without unconditional surrender. We view *gentleness* as a law to be obeyed, a forced limitation on our behavior, rather than as a character quality God is working into our lives.

How are you doing? Do you see gentleness, power under control, evidenced in your own life? Or is your life characterized by either explosions of anger or pathetic mildness that never gets angry about anything? Both extremes miss the mark. Christians are to be gentle, demonstrating power under the control of God.

Blessed are the gentle, for they shall inherit the earth. We are joint heirs of God, joint heirs with Christ. We will inherit what He inherits:

the whole world. We will be a kingdom of priests who will reign on the earth with Him. Isn't that amazing?

Spend some time in prayer. Do you need to surrender your will to God and be counted among those who are blessed?

Righteousness. The word itself can make us a little uncomfortable. We don't use it much, except perhaps in a negative sense, as in *self-righteous*. Somehow the word *righteousness* feels out of place in our culture. Should it be this way?

We have already learned that Jesus used words in ways that are a little different from what we normally think of. This week we will study the next two beatitudes dealing with righteousness and mercy. You may be surprised at what you see.

OBSERVE

Leader: Read Matthew 5:6 aloud. Have the group say aloud and...

- *draw a box around the word* **blessed:**

  ☐

- *mark the word* **righteousness** *with a big* **R.**

MATTHEW 5:6

Blessed are those who hunger and thirst for righteousness, for they shall be satisfied.

DISCUSS

- Who will be blessed, according to this verse?

- What specific blessing is promised here?

INSIGHT

The word for *righteousness* in the Greek is used to describe whatever is right or just in itself and which therefore conforms to the revealed will of God.

Hunger and *thirst* are bodily cravings that must be satisfied. Life cannot be sustained by simply eating one meal or having an occasional sip of water; rather, the intake of food and water is to be a continual habit of life. So, too, a hunger and thirst for righteousness implies a craving that has to be satisfied, no matter the cost.

To *be satisfied* is to have a deep inner contentment.

• Discuss what Jesus' choice of the words *hunger* and *thirst* tell you about the desires of a true believer.

• Are you satisfied? If not, could it be you are hungry for the wrong things? Are you looking for satisfaction in all the wrong places?

OBSERVE

Leader: Read John 7:37–38 aloud.

• *Have the group underline the phrase* ***if anyone is thirsty.***

DISCUSS

• What insight do these verses give you with respect to hungering and thirsting after righteousness? What will satisfy that craving?

• Think about it. What is it that you just absolutely have to have? What do you hunger for? Thirst for?

JOHN 7:37–38

37 Now on the last day, the great day of the feast, Jesus stood and cried out, saying, "If anyone is thirsty, let him come to Me and drink.

38 "He who believes in Me, as the Scripture said, 'From his innermost being will flow rivers of living water.'"

• Is there anything in your life that might ruin your appetite for righteousness? Think about it, be as specific as possible. If you feel led to, share with the class what God is showing you.

• How would the world be impacted if all believers burned with a desire for God's justice? If all truly desired to live life as God intended it to be lived?

MATTHEW 6:31–33

31 Do not worry then, saying, "What will we eat?" or "What will we drink?" or "What will we wear for clothing?"

32 For the Gentiles eagerly seek all these things; for your heavenly Father knows that you need all these things.

OBSERVE

Is satisfaction—that sense of deep inner contentment—something we can pursue and gain as an end in itself, or is it a by-product of something else?

Leader: Read Matthew 6:31–33 aloud. Have the group...
  • *mark every reference to **your heavenly Father**, including pronouns, with a triangle:* △
  • *mark the word **righteousness** with a big* **R**

DISCUSS

• What are believers to seek, and what will be the result?

• How does this relate to Jesus' promise of satisfying those who hunger and thirst for righteousness?

OBSERVE

How can you be sure you have a genuine hunger and thirst for righteousness?

Leader: Read aloud Psalm 119:1–8, 40, and 123. Have the group…
  • *draw a box around each occurrence of the word **blessed**.*
  • *circle all synonyms for **the Word of God**, such as **law of the Lord, testimonies, precepts, statutes,** etc.*

DISCUSS

• What did you learn about those who are blessed and their relationship to God and His Word?

33 But seek first His kingdom and His righteousness, and all these things will be added to you.

PSALM 119:1–8, 40, 123

1 How blessed are those whose way is blameless, who walk in the law of the LORD.

2 How blessed are those who observe His testimonies, who seek Him with all their heart.

3 They also do no unrighteousness; they walk in His ways.

4 You have ordained Your precepts, that we should keep them diligently.

5 Oh that my ways may be established to keep Your statutes!

6 Then I shall not be ashamed when I look upon all Your commandments.

7 I shall give thanks to You with uprightness of heart, when I learn Your righteous judgments.

8 I shall keep Your statutes; do not forsake me utterly!…

40 Behold, I long for Your precepts; revive me through Your righteousness.…

123 My eyes fail with longing for Your salvation and for Your righteous word.

• Make a list of the ways we are to respond to God's Word if we want to be blessed.

• According to verse 40, what is the psalmist's relationship to God's Word?

• What about you? Are these attitudes characteristic of you?

OBSERVE

As we come to the fifth beatitude you will notice that some of the remaining beatitudes suggest a horizontal, people-to-people aspect to being blessed. How do those who are poor in Spirit, who hunger and thirst for righteousness, respond to others?

MATTHEW 5:7

Blessed are the merciful, for they shall receive mercy.

Leader: Read Matthew 5:7 aloud. Have the group...
- *draw a box around the word **blessed.***
- *mark the words **merciful** and **mercy** with a big **M.***

DISCUSS

• Who will be blessed, according to this verse?

• What is the reward for those who are merciful?

• Is this reward conditional? Explain your answer.

INSIGHT

Mercy refers to an outward manifestation or showing of compassion. The concept of *mercy* assumes two things: first, that there is a need, and second, that you have the ability to meet that need.

2 CORINTHIANS 1:3

Blessed be the God and Father of our Lord Jesus Christ, the Father of mercies and God of all comfort.

EPHESIANS 2:4–7

4 But God, being rich in mercy, because of His great love with which He loved us,

5 even when we were dead in our transgressions, made us alive together with

OBSERVE

Where is mercy found?

Leader: Read 2 Corinthians 1:3 and Ephesians 2:4–7 aloud. Have the group...
- *mark every reference to **God**, including synonyms and pronouns, with a triangle.*
- *mark the words **mercies** and **mercy** with a big **M**.*

DISCUSS

- How is God described in these passages?

• To whom has God shown mercy, according to Ephesians 2?

Christ (by grace you have been saved),

6 and raised us up with Him, and seated us with Him in the heavenly places in Christ Jesus,

• How did He show it?

7 so that in the ages to come He might show the surpassing riches of His grace in kindness toward us in Christ Jesus.

OBSERVE

Since we have received God's amazing mercy, how should we respond to those around us who are difficult to get along with?

Leader: Read Luke 6:35–36 aloud. Have the group…
  • *mark with a triangle every synonym and pronoun referring to God.*
  • *mark each occurrence of the word merciful with a big M.*

LUKE 6:35–36

35 But love your enemies, and do good, and lend, expecting nothing in return; and your reward will be great, and you will be sons of the Most High; for He Himself is kind to ungrateful and evil men.

36 Be merciful, just as your Father is merciful.

DISCUSS

• How are believers to treat their enemies?

• Whose example are we to follow in this?

MATTHEW 9:9–13

9 As Jesus went on from there, He saw a man called Matthew, sitting in the tax collector's booth; and He said to him, "Follow Me!" And he got up and followed Him.

10 Then it happened that as Jesus was reclining at the table in the house, behold, many tax collectors and sinners came and were dining with Jesus and His disciples.

11 When the Pharisees saw this, they said to His disciples, "Why

OBSERVE

Leader: Read Matthew 9:9–13, 12:7, and 23:23 aloud.

   • *Have the group say aloud and mark each reference to **mercy** or **compassion** with a big **M**.*

DISCUSS

• What did you learn from marking *mercy* and *compassion*?

• What role does mercy play in your life?

• What are some practical ways you can show mercy to others?

• Is God more pleased by our gestures of worship or by our treating others with compassion? Explain your answer.

is your Teacher eating with the tax collectors and sinners?"

12 But when Jesus heard this, He said, "It is not those who are healthy who need a physician, but those who are sick.

13 "But go and learn what this means: 'I desire compassion, and not sacrifice,' for I did not come to call the righteous, but sinners."

MATTHEW 12:7

But if you had known what this means, 'I desire compassion, and not a sacrifice,' you would not have condemned the innocent.

MATTHEW 23:23

Woe to you, scribes and Pharisees, hypocrites! For you tithe mint and dill and cummin, and have neglected the weightier provisions of the law: justice and mercy and faithfulness; but these are the things you should have done without neglecting the others.

• Describe a time when another believer treated you with mercy. How did that transform a difficult situation?

WRAP IT UP

Two characteristics of a Christian are a passion for righteousness and compassion for others. Does this describe you? Are you so passionate for righteousness that it consumes your thought life? If not, why not? Does your passion for a right relationship with God translate into a compassion for people?

Studying the Beatitudes can be painful. For most of us, there is a jarring difference between who we actually are and who we should be as followers of Jesus. Some of us would say we have a relationship with God, but we would stop short of saying we thirst for righteousness. We might say we are merciful, but do we reach out in compassion to those who need help?

If the Spirit has convicted you that your life does not look like the description Jesus gave in these opening verses of His Sermon on the Mount, here are some suggestions for a spiritual tune up.

1. **Surrender.** First, start with an unconditional surrender of your will to the will of God. In prayer, commit your will to the Father. You might even pray "Father, not my will but Yours be done."

2. **Make your spiritual life your priority.** As a part of your surrender, tell God you will seek Him daily. Make spending time in the Word of God the daily priority in your life. We at Precept Ministries have several great Bible studies to help you establish yourself in God's Word.

3. **Follow people who are following hard after Christ.** Look around your church for godly mentors. Read the biographies

of godly people. Seeing the passion in their life will fuel the passion in yours.

4. **Ask God** to give you a passion, a hunger, a desperate thirst for righteousness, and compassion for others.

The poor in spirit, those who mourn, the gentle, those who hunger and thirst for righteousness, and the merciful—these are the ones who are blessed of God. The list seems simple and appropriately religious. But as we have seen, the reality Jesus described in the Beatitudes isn't about outward, self-imposed religiosity. His words call us to a radical, supernatural life, a life that can be lived only through the indwelling presence of the Holy Spirit.

This lesson is no different. So be ready to be challenged as we study what it means to be pure in heart and to be a peacemaker.

OBSERVE

Leader: *Read aloud Matthew 5:8. Have the group say aloud and...*

- *draw a box around the word **blessed:***

- *mark the phrase **pure in heart** with a heart:* ♡

MATTHEW 5:8

Blessed are the pure in heart, for they shall see God.

DISCUSS

- Who will be blessed, according to this verse?

- What awaits those who are pure in heart?

ROMANS 3:10–12

10 As it is written, "There is none righteous, not even one;

11 There is none who understands, there is none who seeks for God;

12 All have turned aside, together they have become useless; there is none who does good, there is not even one."

OBSERVE

Is being pure in heart just a matter of being a good person?

Leader: Read Romans 3:10–12 aloud. Have the group...
- *mark **God** with a triangle:* △
- *circle each occurrence of the word **none**.*

DISCUSS

- What did you learn by marking the word *none*?

- Who seeks after God?

- If this is the condition of mankind without Christ, what does that tell you about the state of our hearts?

OBSERVE

Jesus said the pure in heart shall see God. But in light of what we've just read, the question is, how do we get a pure heart?

Leader: Read aloud Jeremiah 31:33, Ezekiel 36:26–27, and Hebrews 10:22 aloud. Have the group...

- *mark every reference to God, including synonyms and pronouns, with a triangle:* △
- *mark heart(s) with a heart:* ♡
- *draw a squiggly line under the word clean, like this:* ∿∿∿

DISCUSS

- Discuss what you learned from marking *God* and *heart(s)*.

- Just so you don't miss it, what do we receive as we enter into the new covenant, this new relationship with God?

- What did you learn about our hearts from Hebrews 10:22?

JEREMIAH 31:33

"But this is the covenant which I will make with the house of Israel after those days," declares the LORD, "I will put My law within them and on their heart I will write it; and I will be their God, and they shall be My people."

EZEKIEL 36:26–27

26 "Moreover, I will give you a new heart and put a new spirit within you; and I will remove the heart of stone from your flesh and give you a heart of flesh.

27 "I will put My Spirit within you and cause you to walk in My statutes, and you will be careful to observe My ordinances."

HEBREWS 10:22

Let us draw near with a sincere heart in full assurance of faith, having our hearts sprinkled clean from an evil conscience and our bodies washed with pure water.

EPHESIANS 5:25–26

25 Husbands, love your wives, just as Christ also loved the church and gave Himself up for her,

26 so that He might sanctify her, having cleansed her by the washing of water with the word.

JOHN 17:17

Sanctify them in the truth; Your word is truth.

• If you are a believer, how does knowing this truth affect the way you live?

• Are you walking in God's statutes? Has your heart been sprinkled clean? Explain your answer.

OBSERVE

Having been cleansed from an evil conscience by the blood of Jesus Christ, how do you stay pure? How do you keep your heart from being stained all over again?

Leader: Read Ephesians 5:25–26 and John 17:17 aloud. Have the group…
- *double underline each occurrence of* **word** *and* **truth**.
- *draw a squiggly line under the words* **cleansed** *and* **sanctify**.

INSIGHT

To *sanctify* is the action of setting apart something as holy.

DISCUSS

• According to Ephesians 5:25–26, how does Jesus sanctify the church?

• What did Jesus request of the Father in John 17:17?

• What is the connection between sanctification—or cleanness—and the word?

• What does this tell you about your need to spend time in the Bible consistently?

1 JOHN 1:9

OBSERVE

Leader: Read 1 John 1:9 aloud. Have the group...

• *mark a slash like this ╱ through each mention of **sins** and **unrighteousness**.*

• *draw a squiggly line under the word **cleanse**.*

If we confess our sins, He [God] is faithful and righteous to forgive us our sins and to cleanse us from all unrighteousness.

DISCUSS

- From what you saw in this verse, in addition to spending time in the Word of God, what is another way to be cleansed?

- Who actually does the cleansing?

INSIGHT

To confess means "to say the same thing, to speak the same word." In other words, confessing our sins means agreeing with God that what we have done is sin.

- From all you have seen so far, what are two things that would keep someone from having an intimate relationship with God? Explain your answer.

OBSERVE

Leader: Read Psalm 24:1–6 aloud. Have the group say aloud and...
- *draw a squiggly line under the words **clean** and **pure**.*
- *draw a box around the word **blessing**.*

DISCUSS

- Who may ascend into the hill of the Lord or stand in His holy place? How is this person described?

- What would be the implications of the phrase clean hands? Pure heart?

- According to verse 5, what will the person with clean hands and a pure heart receive?

PSALM 24:1–6

¹ The earth is the LORD's, and all it contains, the world, and those who dwell in it.

² For He has founded it upon the seas and established it upon the rivers.

³ Who may ascend into the hill of the LORD? And who may stand in His holy place?

⁴ He who has clean hands and a pure heart, who has not lifted up his soul to falsehood and has not sworn deceitfully.

⁵ He shall receive a blessing from the LORD and righteousness from the God of his salvation.

6 This is the generation of those who seek Him, who seek Your face—even Jacob. Selah.

• What about you? Are you able to stand before the Lord with clean hands and a pure heart? If not, what steps do you need to take to do so?

MATTHEW 5:9

Blessed are the peacemakers, for they shall be called sons of God.

OBSERVE

Leader: Read Matthew 5:9 aloud. Have the group...

• *draw a box around the word* **blessed.**

• *mark the word* **peacemakers** *with a big* **P.**

DISCUSS

• Who is blessed, according to Matthew 5:9?

• What is promised to them?

OBSERVE

What makes someone a peacemaker?

Leader: *Read aloud Colossians 1:19–22.*
- *Have the group say aloud and place a check mark like this ✓ over each reference to* **reconcile** *and* **peace.**

DISCUSS

- Who did the reconciling in this passage?

- What was the state of mankind before we were reconciled?

- How were reconciliation and peace made possible?

19 For it was the Father's good pleasure for all the fullness to dwell in Him,

20 and through Him to reconcile all things to Himself, having made peace through the blood of His cross; through Him, I say, whether things on earth or things in heaven.

21 And although you were formerly alienated and hostile in mind, engaged in evil deeds,

22 yet He has now reconciled you in His fleshly body through death, in order to present you before Him holy and blameless and beyond reproach.

ROMANS 5:10–11

10 For if while we were enemies we were reconciled to God through the death of His Son, much more, having been reconciled, we shall be saved by His life.

11 And not only this, but we also exult in God through our Lord Jesus Christ, through whom we have now received the reconciliation.

OBSERVE

In this next passage we see Paul explaining more about how believers have been saved from the wrath of God.

Leader: Read Romans 5:10–11 aloud.

  • *Have the group say aloud and place a check mark like this ✓ over each occurrence of the words* **reconciled** *and* **reconciliation.**

DISCUSS

• What were we when God reconciled us, when He removed the hostility between us and Himself?

• How were we reconciled to God?

• Through whom did we receive this reconciliation?

OBSERVE

What makes you a peacemaker? First, it is having peace with God. Let's see what else is involved in being a peacemaker.

Leader: Read Romans 12:16–18 and 1 Thessalonians 5:12–13 aloud. Have the group...
- *circle each of the pronouns **your** and **you**, which refer to **believers** in this passage.*
- *draw a check mark over each reference to **peace**.*

DISCUSS

• How are believers to be characterized?

• What did you learn about peace from this passage?

ROMANS 12:16–18

16 Be of the same mind toward one another; do not be haughty in mind, but associate with the lowly. Do not be wise in your own estimation.

17 Never pay back evil for evil to anyone. Respect what is right in the sight of all men.

18 If possible, so far as it depends on you, be at peace with all men.

1 THESSALONIANS 5:12–13

12 But we request of you, brethren, that you appreciate those who diligently labor among you, and have charge over you in the Lord and give you instruction,

13 and that you esteem them very highly in love because of their work. Live in peace with one another.

The Greek verb used in the phrase *live in peace* suggests an ongoing condition or action. Believers are commanded to be continually living in peace with one another. The idea is to maintain peace rather than initiate it.

• How are you succeeding as a peacemaker? Are you doing everything you can to maintain the peace in your family? In your church? With your neighbors?

MATTHEW 5:22–24

22 "But I say to you that everyone who is angry with his brother shall be guilty before the court; and whoever says to his brother, 'You good-for-nothing,' shall be guilty before the supreme

OBSERVE

Let's look at what Jesus had to say about living at peace with others.

Leader: Read Matthew 5:22–24 aloud. Have the group…
  • *circle the pronoun **you** when it refers to **Jesus' followers**.*
  • *draw a check mark over the word **reconciled**.*

DISCUSS

• Discuss this passage and how it relates to what we have been learning.

court; and whoever says, 'You fool,' shall be guilty enough to go into the fiery hell.

23 "Therefore if you are presenting your offering at the altar, and there remember that your brother has something against you,

• If you know a brother or sister in Christ has something against you, what is your responsibility as a peacemaker?

24 leave your offering there before the altar and go; first be reconciled to your brother, and then come and present your offering.

• Blessed are the peacemakers! Are you blessed because you are making and keeping peace in the body?

• What is the reward for the peacemaker?

INSIGHT

According to Jewish thought, the word *son* carried the idea of one who bears the characteristics of the father.

• Who do you look like when you are being a peacemaker? How does that translate into the lives of those God has brought into your life?

WRAP IT UP

Blessed by God are the pure in heart and the peacemakers. Perhaps these two characteristics were set next to each other by Jesus on purpose. A pure heart is not simply a sinless one; it is a heart that is both sinless and selfless. A pure heart shines as a light in the darkness. In other words, to be a peacemaker, you need a pure heart, and one who has a pure heart will be a peacemaker.

The best peacemakers are men and women who are at peace with God. When God changes a heart and cleanses us from our selfishness, our *me*-centeredness, it is then that we are able to show the love of God to a chaotic world and be peacemakers. Our priorities have been transformed.

One whose life has been changed, whose heart is pure, should be living a life characterized by the label *peacemaker.* Are you living at peace with those people God brings into your circle of influence? God sometimes brings people into our lives so that we can influence them in the name of Christ. Are you helping the enemies of God see their need to be reconciled to Him? What about peacemaking attitudes and behaviors toward brothers and sisters in Christ?

Finish this week's lesson with a time of prayer, asking God to show you...

- any dirt in your life, anything that you are involved with or holding on to that you need to be cleansed of.
- any area where you are not walking as a peacemaker.

If He reveals anything, anything at all…

- confess it as sin.
- ask Him to forgive you.
- ask Him to re-create in you a clean heart.

Search me, O God, and know my heart;
Try me and know my anxious thoughts;
And see if there be any hurtful way in me,
And lead me in the everlasting way. (Psalm 139:23–24)

A radical Spirit-filled life is going to stand out in this world, just as a light is easily seen shining in the darkness.

The sort of life Jesus describes in the Beatitudes will undoubtedly draw some attention in this world—and not all of it will be positive. The world will not love you. But be encouraged: you are in good company. The world persecuted Jesus also.

OBSERVE

Leader: Read aloud Matthew 5:10–12. Have the group say aloud and...

- *draw a box around the word **blessed:***

- *mark each occurrence of **persecute(d)** with a jagged line, like this:*

DISCUSS

- Who is blessed, according to these verses?

- Why are they being persecuted?

- What form does this persecution take?

- Is persecution of those who follow after God a new thing, according to these verses?

MATTHEW 5:10–12

10 Blessed are those who have been persecuted for the sake of righteousness, for theirs is the kingdom of heaven.

11 Blessed are you when people insult you and persecute you, and falsely say all kinds of evil against you because of Me.

12 Rejoice and be glad, for your reward in heaven is great; for in the same way

they persecuted the prophets who were before you.

• What will be the reward of those who are persecuted for their commitment to righteousness?

PHILIPPIANS 1:27–30

27 Only conduct yourselves in a manner worthy of the gospel of Christ, so that whether I come and see you or remain absent, I will hear of you that you are standing firm in one spirit, with one mind striving together for the faith of the gospel;

28 in no way alarmed by your opponents— which is a sign of destruction for them, but of salvation for you, and that too, from God.

OBSERVE

Let's look at some things we need to know about suffering or persecution.

Leader: Read Philippians 1:27–30 aloud. Have the group…
  • *circle each of the pronouns* ***yourselves*** *and* ***you,*** *which refer to* ***believers*** *in this passage.*
  • *mark the word* ***suffer*** *with a jagged line, like this:* 〰〰

DISCUSS

• From what you read in verse 27, how are we to conduct ourselves?

• What are we to do when we are opposed?

• How are we to respond to our opponents, according to verse 28?

• What does this type of response demonstrate to our opponents? To us?

29 For to you it has been granted for Christ's sake, not only to believe in Him, but also to suffer for His sake,

• According to verse 29, two things have been granted you for Christ's sake. What are they?

30 experiencing the same conflict which you saw in me, and now hear to be in me.

• So should we be caught off guard by persecution? Explain your answer.

OBSERVE

Paul's statement in Philippians about persecution mirrored what Jesus had already told His followers. Let's look at the Savior's words.

Leader: Read John 15:18–20 aloud. Have the group...

> • *draw a big* **X** *over the words* **hates** *and* **hated.**
>
> • *mark each reference to* **persecute(d)** *with a jagged line.*

JOHN 15:18–20

18 If the world hates you, you know that it has hated Me before it hated you.

19 If you were of the world, the world would love its own; but because you are not of the world, but I chose you out of the world, because of this the world hates you.

20 Remember the word that I said to you, "A slave is not greater than his master." If they persecuted Me, they will also persecute you; if they kept My word, they will keep yours also.

DISCUSS

• What did you learn from marking *hates* and *hated*?

• What did you learn from marking the references to persecution?

1 THESSALONIANS 3:3–4

3 so that no one would be disturbed by these afflictions; for you yourselves know that we have been destined for this.

4 For indeed when we were with you, we kept telling you in advance that we were going to suffer affliction; and so it came to pass, as you know.

OBSERVE

The first three chapters of Thessalonians give us an account of what happened when Paul went to Thessalonica to deliver the gospel. Paul taught the new converts what to expect in their new life.

Leader: Read 1 Thessalonians 3:3–4 aloud.
  • *Have the group say aloud and mark each reference to **affliction(s)** with a jagged line.*

DISCUSS

• What warning did Paul give to the Thessalonians?

• Does your church teach this? Do you believe it? Is it an integral part of your witnessing and discipling?

OBSERVE

Let's look at some words on affliction from one of the disciples who witnessed Jesus' suffering firsthand.

Leader: Read 1 Peter 4:12–16 aloud. Have the group...

• *mark a jagged line over every reference to* **suffering***, including synonyms such as* **fiery ordeal** *and* **reviled***.*
• *draw a box around the word* **blessed***.*

DISCUSS

• Discuss what you learned about suffering from this passage.

• What do you think Peter meant when he wrote about degrees of suffering in verse 13? Explain your answer.

1 PETER 4:12–16

12 Beloved, do not be surprised at the fiery ordeal among you, which comes upon you for your testing, as though some strange thing were happening to you;

13 but to the degree that you share the sufferings of Christ, keep on rejoicing, so that also at the revelation of His glory you may rejoice with exultation.

14 If you are reviled for the name of Christ, you are blessed, because the Spirit of glory and of God rests on you.

15 Make sure that none of you suffers as a murderer, or thief, or evildoer, or a troublesome meddler;

16 but if anyone suffers as a Christian, he is not to be ashamed, but is to glorify God in this name.

• Does all suffering bring honor to God? Look closely at verse 15 and explain your answer.

• Are you suffering for the gospel? Had anyone warned you to expect this? How does knowing these truths help you?

---

2 TIMOTHY 3:12

Indeed, all who desire to live godly in Christ Jesus will be persecuted.

OBSERVE

Leader: Read 2 Timothy 3:12 aloud.
  • *Have the group say the word **persecuted** and mark it with a jagged line.*

DISCUSS

• Who will be persecuted?

• Are you being persecuted? If not, perhaps you need to take a serious look at your life. Are you honoring God and pursuing righteousness in ways that mark you as being set apart for Him?

OBSERVE

We've seen that suffering is a certainty for the child of God. Now let's look together at some other things we need to know about suffering and persecution.

Leader: Read Romans 8:16–17 aloud. Have the group…
- *circle the phrases* **children of God** *and* **heirs of God.**
- *mark the word* **suffer** *with a jagged line.*

DISCUSS
- What is suffering a mark of?

- What is the relationship between suffering and glorification?

ROMANS 8:16–17

16 The Spirit Himself testifies with our spirit that we are children of God,

17 and if children, heirs also, heirs of God and fellow heirs with Christ, if indeed we suffer with Him so that we may also be glorified with Him.

1 PETER 1:6–7

6 In this you greatly rejoice, even though now for a little while, if necessary, you have been distressed by various trials,

7 so that the proof of your faith, being more precious than gold which is perishable, even though tested by fire, may be found to result in praise and glory and honor at the revelation of Jesus Christ.

OBSERVE

Leader: *Read 1 Peter 1:6–7 aloud.*

• *Have the group say and mark the words* **trials** *and* **tested** *with a big* **T.**

DISCUSS

• What did you learn from marking *trials* and *tested*?

• How does suffering result in glory?

1 PETER 2:18–25

18 Servants, be submissive to your masters with all respect, not only to those who are good and gentle, but also to those who are unreasonable.

OBSERVE

Leader: *Read 1 Peter 2:18–25 aloud.*

• *Have the group mark every reference to* **suffering** *with a jagged line.*

DISCUSS

• What kind of suffering finds favor with God?

• Who is our example of suffering, according to verse 21?

INSIGHT

The Greek word for *example* refers to an outline, a drawing, or a copy book of letters to be used by the pupil as a model to follow.

• In 1 Peter 2:21–25 Peter gave believers a pattern to follow when we suffer. Make a list of the characteristics and behaviors you see in this pattern.

• Since suffering is certain, how are we to respond to those who cause our suffering? Explain your answer.

19 For this finds favor, if for the sake of conscience toward God a person bears up under sorrows when suffering unjustly.

20 For what credit is there if, when you sin and are harshly treated, you endure it with patience? But if when you do what is right and suffer for it you patiently endure it, this finds favor with God.

21 For you have been called for this purpose, since Christ also suffered for you, leaving you an example for you to follow in His steps,

22 who committed no sin, nor was any deceit found in His mouth;

23 and while being reviled, He did not revile in return; while suffering, He uttered no threats, but kept entrusting Himself to Him who judges righteously;

24 and He Himself bore our sins in His body on the cross, so that we might die to sin and live to righteousness; for by His wounds you were healed.

25 For you were continually straying like sheep, but now you have returned to the Shepherd and Guardian of your souls.

• Jesus trusted in His Father, the One who would righteously judge His tormentors. One of the benefits of persecution is intimate communion with God, because it prompts us to rely on Him. What about you? Are you trusting in your Father? Who do you run to in times of persecution?

• By patiently enduring persecution, you testify to the reality of your faith in Jesus Christ. What kind of impact could that have on those around you?

• Jesus took the persecution; He was willing to endure it. What about you? Are you enduring it or are you fleeing from it? What does your response to unfair criticism and scorn reveal about your faith?

WRAP IT UP

God tells us through the apostle Paul that the gift of faith in Christ and the gift of suffering come together. Your endurance of persecution becomes a testimony to the reality of your faith.

When you stand in front of your opponents and are not alarmed, that's a sign of your salvation. You realize you have a home in heaven. When your opponents see you standing firm without being shaken, they panic. It's like getting into a fight with someone who is not afraid of pain; there is nothing you can do to scare him.

Are you being persecuted for righteousness' sake? Do people mock you or drag your name through the mud because of your relationship with the Lord? If not, could it possibly be that you are not all you ought to be for Him? Could it be you have compromised your standard of righteousness? Are you so like the world that your life doesn't expose their sin, therefore they feel comfortable with you? Or are you so isolated in your own little Christian bubble that you aren't stepping out into the world to be a peacemaker, to show others their need to be reconciled to God?

You've no need to fear when persecution or suffering come into your life. Remember: God is sovereign, He is in control, God holds you in His hand (John 10:28–30), and God is love. He will never permit any suffering you cannot handle, and in handling it you will testify to the reality of your faith in Jesus Christ.

The Beatitudes begin and end with a promise: "theirs is the kingdom of heaven." Therefore, everything in between is included. It's a package deal. When you turn your heart toward God, these attitudes will become apparent in your life. They are the mark of a true believer—one who possesses the full favor of God.

What greater blessing could there be?

40 MINUTE BIBLE STUDIES

No-Homework
That Help You

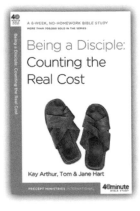

A 6-WEEK, NO-HOMEWORK BIBLE STUDY
MORE THAN 700,000 SOLD IN THE SERIES

Being a Disciple:
Counting the
Real Cost

Kay Arthur, Tom & Jane Hart

PRECEPT MINISTRIES INTERNATIONAL

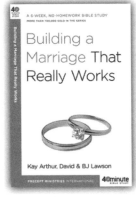

A 6-WEEK, NO-HOMEWORK BIBLE STUDY
MORE THAN 700,000 SOLD IN THE SERIES

Building a
Marriage That
Really Works

Kay Arthur, David & BJ Lawson

PRECEPT MINISTRIES INTERNATIONAL

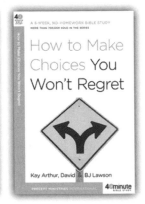

A 6-WEEK, NO-HOMEWORK BIBLE STUDY
MORE THAN 700,000 SOLD IN THE SERIES

How to Make
Choices You
Won't Regret

Kay Arthur, David & BJ Lawson

PRECEPT MINISTRIES INTERNATIONAL

A 6-WEEK, NO-HOMEWORK BIBLE STUDY
MORE THAN 700,000 SOLD IN THE SERIES

A Man's Strategy
For Conquering
Temptation

Bob Vereen

PRECEPT MINISTRIES INTERNATIONAL

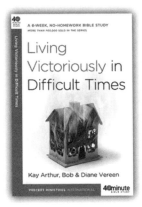

A 6-WEEK, NO-HOMEWORK BIBLE STUDY
MORE THAN 700,000 SOLD IN THE SERIES

Living
Victoriously in
Difficult Times

Kay Arthur, Bob & Diane Vereen

PRECEPT MINISTRIES INTERNATIONAL

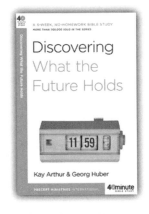

A 6-WEEK, NO-HOMEWORK BIBLE STUDY
MORE THAN 700,000 SOLD IN THE SERIES

Discovering
What the
Future Holds

Kay Arthur & Georg Huber

PRECEPT MINISTRIES INTERNATIONAL

A 6-WEEK, NO-HOMEWORK BIBLE STUDY
MORE THAN 700,000 SOLD IN THE SERIES

Living Like
You Belong
to God

Kay Arthur, David & BJ Lawson

PRECEPT MINISTRIES INTERNATIONAL

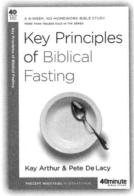

A 6-WEEK, NO-HOMEWORK BIBLE STUDY
MORE THAN 700,000 SOLD IN THE SERIES

Key Principles
of Biblical
Fasting

Kay Arthur & Pete De Lacy

PRECEPT MINISTRIES INTERNATIONAL

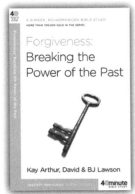

A 6-WEEK, NO-HOMEWORK BIBLE STUDY
MORE THAN 700,000 SOLD IN THE SERIES

Forgiveness:
Breaking the
Power of the Past

Kay Arthur, David & BJ Lawson

PRECEPT MINISTRIES INTERNATIONAL

Bible Studies
Discover Truth For Yourself

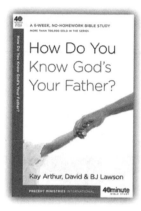

A 6-WEEK, NO-HOMEWORK BIBLE STUDY
MORE THAN 700,000 SOLD IN THE SERIES

How Do You Know God's Your Father?

Kay Arthur, David & BJ Lawson

PRECEPT MINISTRIES INTERNATIONAL · 40minute BIBLE STUDY

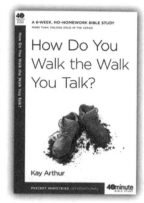

A 6-WEEK, NO-HOMEWORK BIBLE STUDY
MORE THAN 700,000 SOLD IN THE SERIES

How Do You Walk the Walk You Talk?

Kay Arthur

PRECEPT MINISTRIES INTERNATIONAL · 40minute BIBLE STUDY

A 6-WEEK, NO-HOMEWORK BIBLE STUDY
MORE THAN 700,000 SOLD IN THE SERIES

Money and Possessions: The Quest for Contentment

Kay Arthur & David Arthur

PRECEPT MINISTRIES INTERNATIONAL · 40minute BIBLE STUDY

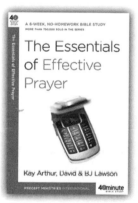

A 6-WEEK, NO-HOMEWORK BIBLE STUDY
MORE THAN 700,000 SOLD IN THE SERIES

The Essentials of Effective Prayer

Kay Arthur, David & BJ Lawson

PRECEPT MINISTRIES INTERNATIONAL · 40minute BIBLE STUDY

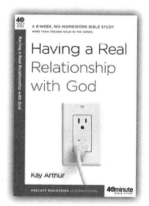

A 6-WEEK, NO-HOMEWORK BIBLE STUDY
MORE THAN 700,000 SOLD IN THE SERIES

Having a Real Relationship with God

Kay Arthur

PRECEPT MINISTRIES INTERNATIONAL · 40minute BIBLE STUDY

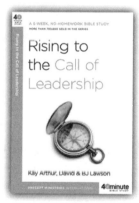

A 6-WEEK, NO-HOMEWORK BIBLE STUDY
MORE THAN 700,000 SOLD IN THE SERIES

Rising to the Call of Leadership

Kay Arthur, David & BJ Lawson

PRECEPT MINISTRIES INTERNATIONAL · 40minute BIBLE STUDY

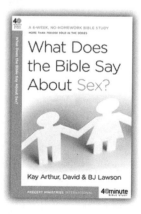

A 6-WEEK, NO-HOMEWORK BIBLE STUDY
MORE THAN 700,000 SOLD IN THE SERIES

What Does the Bible Say About Sex?

Kay Arthur, David & BJ Lawson

PRECEPT MINISTRIES INTERNATIONAL · 40minute BIBLE STUDY

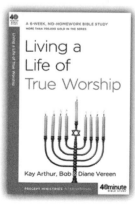

A 6-WEEK, NO-HOMEWORK BIBLE STUDY
MORE THAN 700,000 SOLD IN THE SERIES

Living a Life of True Worship

Kay Arthur, Bob & Diane Vereen

PRECEPT MINISTRIES INTERNATIONAL · 40minute BIBLE STUDY

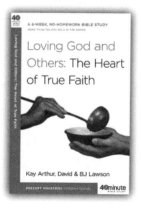

A 6-WEEK, NO-HOMEWORK BIBLE STUDY
MORE THAN 700,000 SOLD IN THE SERIES

Loving God and Others: The Heart of True Faith

Kay Arthur, David & BJ Lawson

PRECEPT MINISTRIES INTERNATIONAL · 40minute BIBLE STUDY

Another powerful study series
from beloved Bible teacher

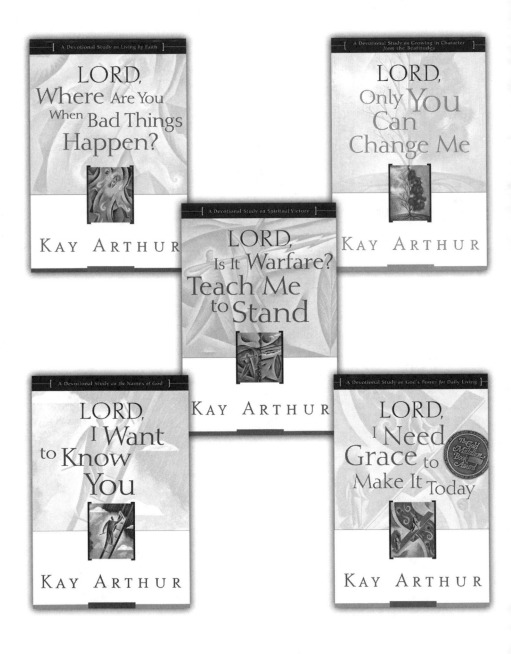

KAY ARTHUR

The Lord series provides insightful, warm-hearted Bible studies designed to meet you where you are—and help you discover God's answers to your deepest needs.

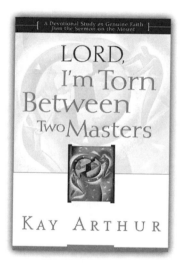

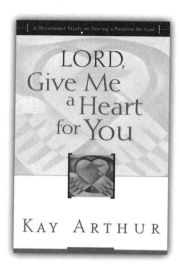

ABOUT KAY ARTHUR AND PRECEPT MINISTRIES INTERNATIONAL

KAY ARTHUR is known around the world as an international Bible teacher, author, conference speaker, and host of the national radio and television programs *Precepts for Life,* which reaches a worldwide viewing audience of over 94 million. A four-time Gold Medallion Award–winning author, Kay has authored more than 100 books and Bible studies.

Kay and her husband, Jack, founded Precept Ministries International in 1970 in Chattanooga, Tennessee, with a vision to establish people in God's Word. Today, the ministry has a worldwide outreach. In addition to inductive study training workshops and thousands of small-group studies across America, PMI reaches nearly 150 countries with inductive Bible studies translated into nearly 70 languages, teaching people to discover Truth for themselves.

Contact Precept Ministries International for more information about inductive Bible studies in your area.

Precept Ministries International
P.O. Box 182218
Chattanooga, TN 37422-7218
800-763-8280
www.precept.org

ABOUT DAVID AND BJ LAWSON

DAVID AND BJ LAWSON have been involved with Precept Ministries International since 1980. After nine years in the pastorate, they joined PMI full-time as directors of the student ministries and staff teachers and trainers. A featured speaker at PMI conferences and in Precept Upon Precept videos, David writes for the Precept Upon Precept series, the New Inductive Study Series, and the 40-Minute Bible Studies series. BJ has written numerous 40-Minute Bible Studies and serves as the chief editor and developer of the series. In addition she is a featured speaker at PMI women's conferences.